PRE-SCHOOL COLOURS AND SHAPES

Fun-filled Activities

Om KIDZ
An imprint of Om Books International

Red

Little Red Riding Hood is going to meet her grandma. Circle (O) the red things that you see in the picture.

How many did you find? Name them.

Red

Jingle bells, jingle bells! Colour Santa's  red and help him get ready.

Trace and write red with a .

red red red red

Green

Mr Bear opens the box. Up pops the green frog! Circle (O) all the green things in the picture.

How many did you find? Name them.

Green

The bunnies want to decorate the tree. Colour the  green for them.

Trace and write green with a .

green green green

Yellow

Quack Quack! The bright yellow sun is back. Circle (O) the yellow things in the picture.

How many did you find? Name them.

Yellow

The animals are off to school. Colour their 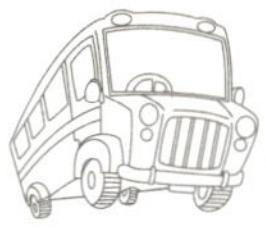 yellow and make it bright.

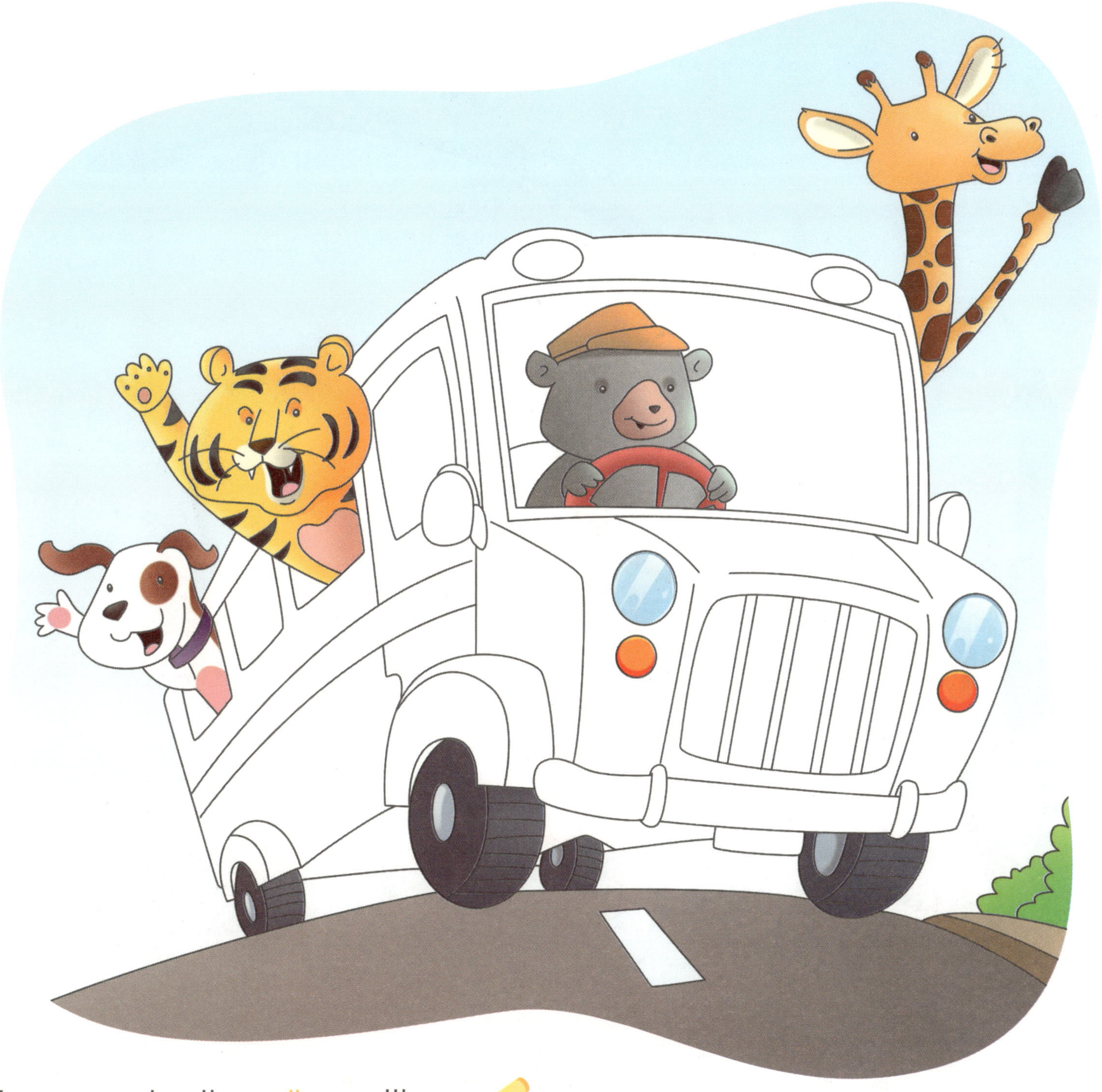

Trace and write yellow with a 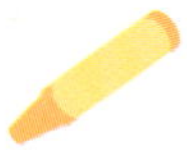.

yellow yellow yellow

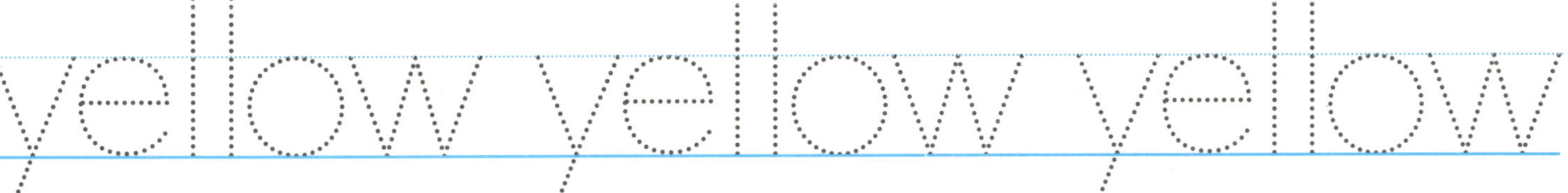

Blue

Miss Birdie is busy painting. Can you find and circle (O) the things that are blue in the picture?

How many did you find? Name them.

Blue

What a fun ride it is! There's more to do! Colour the  blue.

Trace and write blue with a .

blue blue blue blue

Orange

The bear with orange shades! The penguin and the bear are having a nice time playing.

Circle (O) the orange things in the picture.

How many did you find? Name them.

Orange

A yummy treat for Jimmy! Colour the  orange before it melts!

Trace and write orange with a .

orange orange

Brown

Jack bakes a brown cake! Identify and circle (O) all the brown things in the picture.

How many did you find? Name them.

Brown

Click, Click! Chatter the monkey is ready for a click. Colour the  brown.

Trace and write brown with a .

brown brown brown

Black

It's Kim's ride on the wheels! Circle (O) the **black** things that you see in the picture.

How many did you find? Name them.

Black

Miss Tig with a wig! Colour her   **black** to complete the picture.

Trace and write **black** with a .

black black black

Fun Time!

Let's work together! The ducks are busy building their home. Colour the picture beautifully for them.

Circle

High we shall fly with the big circle! Trace the circles and colour them to complete the picture.

Oval

Soon, the oval buds will bloom! Trace the oval shaped things in the picture and colour them.

Triangle

It's time to have the tangy triangle sandwich! Trace the triangles in the picture and colour them.

It's good morning on the Diamond Farm. Trace the diamonds in the picture and colour them.

Square

Little elf is ready with the Christmas presents and is waiting at the square. Trace all the squares and colour them to complete the picture.

Rectangle

Mr Patt with a rectangular hat! Trace the rectangles in the picture and colour them.

Fun Time!

It's time for a splash! Pog is having an awesome time at the beach.

Count the ● and ▲ shapes in the picture.

How many did you find? Circle the number.

▲	1	2	3	4	5	6	7	8	9	10
●	1	2	3	4	5	6	7	8	9	10

Count the Shapes

Let's have a cool break! Count the 🟦 and 🟧 shapes in the picture.

How many did you find? Circle the number.

🟦	1	2	3	4	5	6	7	8	9	10
🟧	1	2	3	4	5	6	7	8	9	10

Count the Shapes

It's time for a puppet show! Count the shapes you see.

How many did you find? Write the correct number for each.

Colour the Shapes

Colour the shapes according to the given key.

 = blue

 = green

 = red

 = orange

 = yellow

 = brown

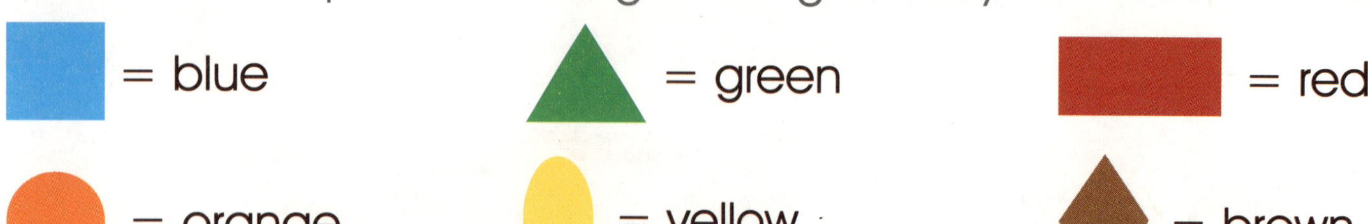

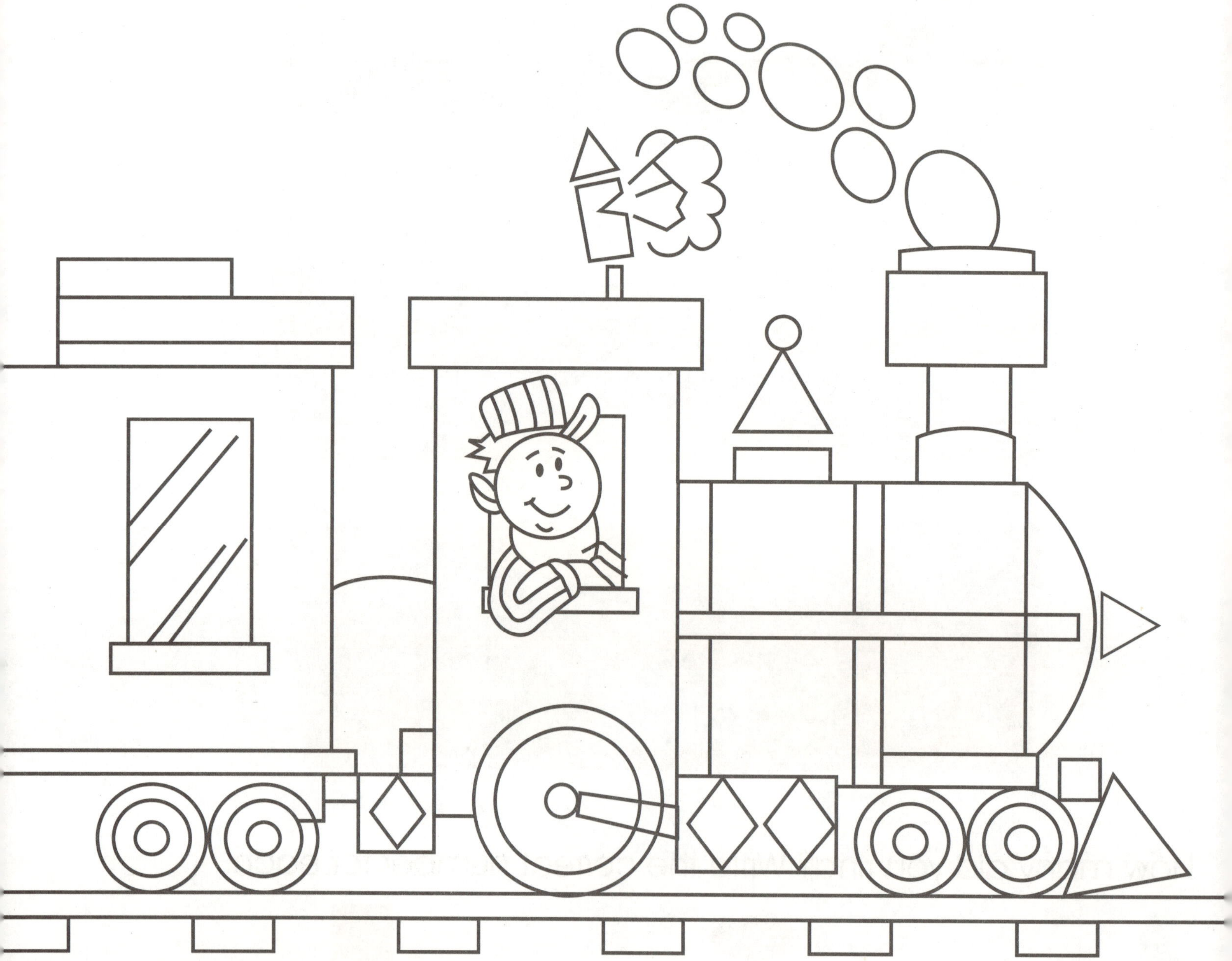

Fun Time!

Colour the turtle and fish .

Colour the Picture

Cheeky and Squeaky in the rain! Colour the picture beautifully.

Review Time!

Join the dots and draw the shapes. Then name each shape.

Review Time!

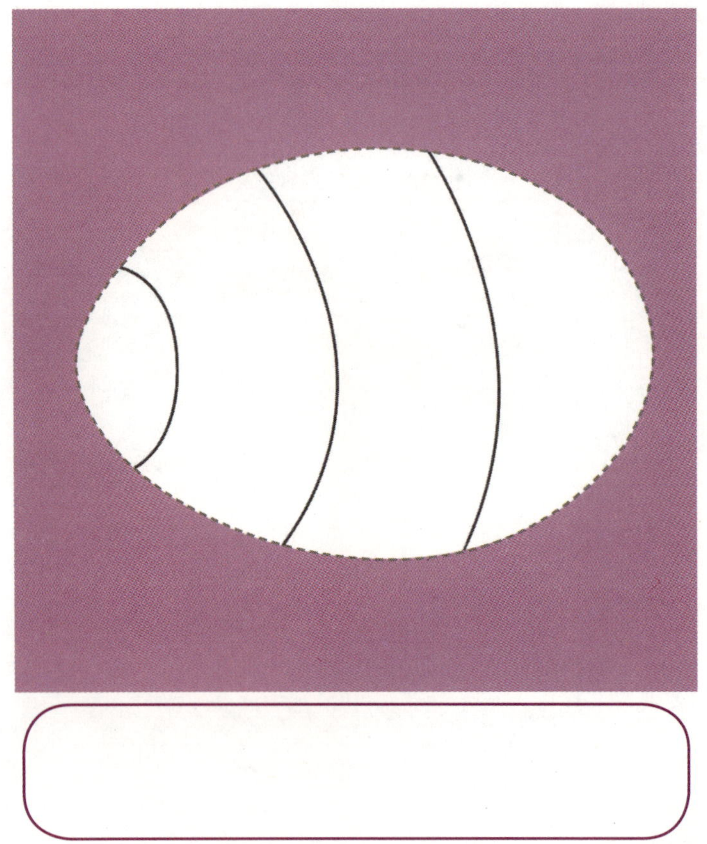

Colour the Picture

What are the kids watching on the television?

Colour the places with dots yellow and find it.

Answer key

Page 2

Page 3

Children will do on their own.

Page 4

Page 5

Children will do on their own.

Page 6

Page 7

Children will do on their own.

Page 8

Page 9

Children will do on their own.

Page 10

Page 11

Children will do on their own.

Page 12

Page 13

Children will do on their own.

Page 14

Page 15-22

Children will do on their own.

Page 23

Circle number 7

Circle number 4

Page 24

Circle number 10

Circle number 6

Page 25

Shape	Number
Triangle	4
Square	5
Oval	3
Circle	2
Square	1
 Trapezium	1

Page 26-31

Children will do on their own.